EXPLORING
THEATER

Producing in Theater

Daniel E. Harmon

Cavendish
Square

New York

Published in 2017 by Cavendish Square Publishing, LLC
243 5th Avenue, Suite 136, New York, NY 10016

First Edition

Website: cavendishsq.com

This publication represents the opinions and views of the author based on his or her personal experience, knowledge, and research. The information in this book serves as a general guide only. The author and publisher have used their best efforts in preparing this book and disclaim liability rising directly or indirectly from the use and application of this book.

CPSIA Compliance Information: Batch #CW17CSQ

All websites were available and accurate when this book was sent to press.

Cataloging-in-Publication Data

Names: Harmon, Daniel E.
Title: Producing in theater / Daniel E. Harmon.
Description: New York : Cavendish Square Publishing, 2017. | Series: Exploring theater | Includes index.
Identifiers: ISBN 9781502622815 (library bound) | ISBN 9781502622822 (ebook)
Subjects: LCSH: Theater--Production and direction--Juvenile literature.
Classification: LCC PN2053.H37 2017 | DDC 792.02'32--dc23

Editorial Director: David McNamara
Editor: Fletcher Doyle
Copy Editor: Nathan Heidelberger
Associate Art Director: Amy Greenan
Designer: Jessica Nevins
Production Coordinator: Karol Szymczuk
Photo Research: J8 Media

The photographs in this book are used by permission and through the courtesy of: Cover Walter McBride/Getty Images; p. 4 Brent N. Clarke/FilmMagic/Getty Images; p. 6 Jason Lindsey/Alamy Stock Photo; pp. 9, 13, 19, 21, 51 ZUMA Press Inc/Alamy Stock Photo; p. 11 Rawpixel.com/Shutterstock.com; p. 16 Hill Street Studios/Blend Images/Getty Images; p. 23 Visivasnc/iStockphoto.com; p. 28 Kamira/Shutterstock.com; p. 30 Thierry Orban/Sygma/Getty Images; p. 32 Peter Bischoff/PB Archive/Getty Images; 34 Jason Davis/Getty Images for Barbershop Harmony Society; p. 42 REUTERS/Alamy Stock Photo; p. 49 Scott Campbell/Alamy Stock Photo; p. 56 Mel Stoutsenberger/Moment/Getty Images; p. 58 Walter McBride/WireImage/Getty Images; p. 60 Bethany Clarke/Getty Images; p. 62 Andre Jenny/Alamy Stock Photo; p. 65 DPA Picture Alliance Archive/Alamy Stock Photo; p. 70 Roibu/iStock/Thinkstock.com; p. 74 John Burke/Stockbyte/Getty Images; p. 76 AberCPC/Alamy Stock Photo; p. 79 Revirado/Alamy Stock Photo; p. 80 Image Source/Photodisc/Getty Images; p. 83 Tinseltown/Shutterstock.com; p. 87 PA Images/Alamy Stock Photo.

Printed in the United States of America

CONTENTS

Actors Bryce Pinkham (*left*) and Jefferson Mays take a curtain call in a New York City presentation of *A Gentleman's Guide to Love and Murder.*

CHAPTER ONE

ATTENTION TO DETAIL

The auditorium lights go down. A moment of expectant silence and inactivity … and then the curtain is raised. The stage bursts alive with a noisome street throng—or materializes subtly with a housekeeper dusting a vase, a child reading a book, or the melancholy lament of a vocalist. During the next two hours, scene by scene, act by act, the audience is drawn through the plot. At the end, if the performance has succeeded, the viewers beam with satisfaction. Intensifying applause greets each successive performer's **curtain call**.

First-time theatergoers, keenly impressed, are bound to wonder: Who was in charge of all this? Whose guiding hand pulled it together? In most community and school theater programs, there is no single guiding force. Each production involves a team. Team leaders have special talents and qualifications.

There always is a director, of course. There is a stage manager. Set and costume designers oversee the work of their separate staffs. Lighting and sound directors coordinate the technical specialists.

Less apparent are the leaders who work year-round to make the theatrical company survive and thrive. They ensure that the program is in the hands of an excellent creative staff. They find funding, control budgets, and oversee marketing and publicity.

The number of details that go into a theatrical production are beyond counting. Theatergoers witness only a small fraction of them during a performance. Those unfamiliar with theater would be surprised to learn how many unseen people are at work and the countless tasks they perform before, during, and after a presentation.

A playwright plots and scripts the play that the company selects to perform. The director works closely with actors, set designers, and behind-the-scenes crews to ensure that the performance is what the playwright envisioned. Designers, artists, carpenters, painters, **riggers**, and other workers create a realistic set with all needed **props**. Costume professionals acquire or create wardrobes for the cast to wear. A lighting designer and experienced electricians create all the lighting effects, while a sound crew operates recorded music, special effects, and amplified sound.

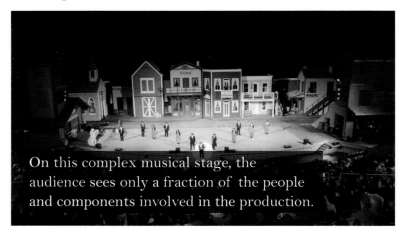

On this complex musical stage, the audience sees only a fraction of the people and components involved in the production.

With all of this going on before and during the show, how is it managed smoothly? Who and what are involved in theatrical production?

What Is a Producer?

It is interesting to contrast production roles in community theater with those in **commercial** entertainment. Movies, television programs and documentaries, and musical recording projects all have designated producers. Their responsibilities vary, depending on the type of production and what it requires. Some producers work for production or recording companies. Others work independently.

Usually, the film/television producer decides on the script or original work on which the project will be based. The producer selects the director, editor, screenwriter, and other key personnel. The producer also secures money for the project. In major undertakings, the producer may be assisted by an executive producer, unit production managers, and other supervisors. After filming, the producer oversees the cutting of scenes, alterations in the music, and other changes as the film or show is readied for release.

The role of a recording producer is similar. The producer selects the songs and session musicians and handles contracts and schedules. In addition, the recording producer functions much like a director in films, instructing the performers and suggesting changes in the musical arrangements. Large-scale recording projects often have an executive producer to take care of business arrangements and a musical producer to oversee creative refinements.

These basic job descriptions are similar to that of the producer in professional theaters. The producer brings all the components together and handles the finances. The producer rents or leases the building, scenery, furniture, and props; buys rights to perform the play; and contracts with a director, cast members, designers, and stage crews. A large production may call for two or more producers.

In some regional professional theaters, the producer's duties are assumed by a managing director and an artistic director. The managing director makes business decisions and handles financial matters. The artistic director makes artistic decisions, including the selection of the director, cast, and designers.

Most community and school theaters differ in organizational structure from commercial entertainment companies in one important way: production responsibilities almost invariably are divided. Different people take charge of the business and creative aspects.

That means different skill sets apply to the various roles. Young people who are interested in serious theater involvement can begin to develop those skills by obtaining experience and training while in high school or junior high. They also can study subjects that indirectly relate to theater.

Production Leaders

The community theater or school theater department may have a production committee or board of directors who make general decisions. They might have an individual designated as the chief administrative officer, managing director, or executive director. This person, as defined by the American Association of Community Theatre, functions as "the guiding force of the organization." Most of the tasks that are assumed by a producer in professional companies usually are the responsibilities of the small theater's artistic director or production manager.

In his acclaimed encyclopedic work *Theatre Craft*, John Caird summarizes the basic difference between production in community/school theater and professional theater. He writes, "In the subsidized [nonprofit] sector, the administrators, Artistic Directors, General Managers or General Directors look after the business of things, but in the commercial theatre where nothing comes free, and no one is permanently salaried, the producer is king."

"When I hear 'production,' I don't think of 'producer,'" observes Leslie Hendon, an actress and singer who has taken part in many productions of the Spartanburg Little Theatre in South Carolina. "I think of the production team that gets everything in line to make it into a show."

A director works with cast members during a dress rehearsal for *Metamorphoses* in a middle school theater project.

She cites the key leaders in each play her organization produces. They include the director or artistic director, stage manager, technical director, set designer, costume designer, and, if it's a musical, the musical director.

Jay Coffman, executive artistic director of the Spartanburg Little Theatre, elaborates, "The 'producer' is actually the organization in general. The financing of a production comes through planning and **budgeting**. In our organization, the producing responsibilities lie with the executive artistic director (sometimes these positions are separate—an executive director and an artistic director). This person is responsible for budgeting for each production and for coming up with a season schedule, which is approved by a board of directors. They are also responsible for contracting the main members of the production staff, including the music director and choreographer and guest directors.

"Additionally, on staff we have a production manager who is responsible for organizing various aspects of the production and for coordinating contracted and volunteer staff, such as costume coordinators, stage managers, and backstage crew."

College theatrical programs have somewhat different producing structures. Jimm Cox, director of theater at the University of South Carolina Upstate, explains, "In academic theater, we seldom have an actual producer, as the responsibilities for that function must be assumed by a faculty member. A program chair normally submits and manages budgets and payments. If there are special needs, the faculty assume that responsibility."

By contrast, Cox adds, "Community theaters sometimes have producers, but the function of that person varies from company to company. Specific fundraising or donations from special sponsors usually fall under the responsibilities of the producer. Most companies do not consider the producer to be part of the creative team, but rather part of the management team. For some companies, the producer or producers are actually financing the production themselves."

Dr. Tim Baxter-Ferguson, director of theater and musical theater at Limestone College, is busy year-round at work in theatrical **venues** on and off campus. He explains how the "producer" role varies: "The term is a little confusing. For college/university theater, all productions are usually overseen by the chair of the department, who will guide a committee that chooses the season, assigns directors and designers, etc. The technical director of the department will oversee all of the technical elements (usually lights, sets, props, and sound). The costumer oversees costumes and makeup. The director oversees the actors and

Some theater companies have administrative structures that include oversight committees.

rehearsals. Everyone answers to the chair, who, of course, answers to the division chair and then to the college president.

"For community theaters there is usually an artistic director who oversees all of the above but answers to a board of directors. Regional theaters operate much the same way."

What Makes a Good Production Leader?

For a small theatrical organization's artistic director, stage manager, or managing director, the first important character trait is sublime confidence. The manager or coordinator must be cool under complex and unforeseen pressures that likely will intensify as show time approaches.

Each production leader must have a fundamental understanding of literally every aspect of theater. All production leaders should be able to anticipate the basic needs of one another. Problem-solving skills are vital. When problems arise, the leaders must help those who work under them resolve the issues quickly and effectively.

Production leaders must be good organizers. They divide the work, appoint individuals to carry out each task, monitor schedules, and oversee their staffs from preproduction through postproduction.

Developing Skills in High School

Only a fraction of high school students will consider pursuing a career in stage or screen acting. A much smaller number will take a career interest in the production aspects of theater. If they do want to become involved, they can benefit early by taking creative arts classes and participating in their schools' drama programs.

The drama program is the obvious first opportunity for students to begin learning about stage production and to experience the excitement of theater. They begin to understand the complexities of what's involved onstage and offstage. They get a sense of whether theater is something they may want to pursue seriously, either as a vocation or an **avocation**. In any case, they are almost sure to enjoy the experience.

Meanwhile, they should consider how their nontheatrical talents and interests can dovetail into theater-related vocations or avocations. Gifted artists can become scenic painters. Young people with computer, electrical, and carpentry skills are in demand for technical assistance in school and community drama productions; commercial

At a California arts academy, a drama teacher breaks the ice on opening day by leading a warm-up game for students.

theater companies will be potential employers later in life. And students with born managerial and administrative instincts will find few arenas where those talents are needed more.

Training After High School

Hundreds of colleges and universities across the country have departments in drama, theater arts, and related studies. Within those programs, numerous majors and study concentrations are offered, from acting to stage production. Students can earn undergraduate and advanced degrees.

Even if they are pursuing other careers, college students interested in engaging in community theater simply as an avocation or occasional pastime can take elective courses to gain formal instruction. It is not difficult to find opportunities close by. Besides major institutions, many community and technical colleges offer theater-related courses.

Some colleges and universities, meanwhile, have established lines of study focusing on various aspects of theater. These will be of most interest to students who are seriously interested in pursuing careers in theatrical production. Here are three examples of college programs with an emphasis on production training:

At Emerson College (Boston, Massachusetts), Stage and Production Management is a specialty **curriculum** within the Department of Performing Arts. In classrooms and on set, students "discover and develop their skills in collaboration, process, and leadership" in theater. The curriculum is intended to "thoroughly prepare you as a stage or production manager." For information, go online to http://www.emerson.edu/performing-arts/undergraduate-programs/stage-production-management.

The School of Drama Graduate Production Technology and Management Option (PTM) at Carnegie Mellon University (Pittsburgh, Pennsylvania) features graduate training programs in technical direction, production, and stage management. The PTM option is designed to provide knowledge of management and technology tools that are available to production leaders who work behind the scenes. It trains students to manage and lead multiple productions and to find creative solutions to problems that arise. Students are engaged in classes and workshops, as well as in stage productions with industry professionals. Details can be found at the program's website: http://www.cmu-drama.com/programs/graduate/grad-ptm.

Columbia University (New York City) offers a master of fine arts degree with a concentration in theater management and producing. The program was developed to train "a new generation of creative managers and producers." It balances studies in professional and nonprofit theaters. Classroom teaching is supervised by NYC-based theater professionals. For more information, visit http://arts.columbia.edu/mfa-theatre-management-producing-concentration.

The majority of participants in community theater, though, have little or no formal training. They learn the ropes by taking on a variety of tasks in school plays and volunteering with a local theater organization. Invariably, they have fun while they learn.

Students construct a stage set for a production following diagrams prepared by the set designer.

CHAPTER TWO
WORKING TOGETHER

The number of individuals required to stage a successful drama, comedy, or musical in community and school theater varies from show to show. The acting cast may be quite small—even solo. Some shows require just two or three workers backstage to set and move furniture and the props. Other scripts involve scores of actors and even more workers behind the scenes. Some call for elaborate special effects, such as the aerial movements of *Peter Pan*. Musical galas typically involve larger casts and crews, sometimes numbering more than one hundred.

Coordinating the efforts of all the players on and offstage falls to the production leaders. Not all of the job titles defined below exist in every theater company, and specific duties vary from one organization to another. But one requirement is universal: the need for carefully orchestrated teamwork. Not only must the production leaders work in union; the individuals working under their supervision must recognize that they all are part of one great team. A careless effort by one person in any department can have a negative ripple effect throughout the company.

Team Captains in Community Theater

Leaders in community theater productions include the production manager, artistic director, director, stage manager, set designer, costume designer, and lighting and sound directors. Unexpected absences caused by illness or personal crisis are not uncommon among the crews and cast. An emergency that takes away one of the leaders can pose a major problem. Here is a list of the directors and what they do.

Artistic Director

The American Association of Community Theatre defines the artistic director's role as "conceiving, developing, and implementing the artistic vision and focus of a theatre company." In some companies, the artistic director also serves as the chief administrative officer. In others, the two positions are separate, although the individuals work closely together.

The artistic director evaluates and appoints the "creative" members of the team in a production. These include the director and set designer. Usually, the artistic director also chooses the stage manager and technical (lighting and sound) director. At least once per season, in most companies, the artistic director directs a play.

This person also is important in public relations. The artistic director speaks to civic groups at every opportunity, is a principal figure at fundraising events, and is always available for comment to the press.

Chief Administrative Officer

Not all community theaters have a chief administrative officer (CAO). The title usually is assigned in larger organizations that have a board of directors. In some, the duties of the CAO are handled by the artistic director, house manager, or a combination of leaders. The person functioning as the CAO also might be called the managing director or executive director.

A CAO prepares the company's annual budget and supervises business affairs. This officer represents the organization in matters such as play **licensing**, insurance, and complying with local government requirements. The CAO has a leadership role in fundraising, grant finding, marketing, and public relations.

Production Manager

Money matters are the primary concern of the production manager. The manager's ultimate

A producer/director (*right*) confers with a stage manager for a local theater company. Successful presentations require close collaboration.

responsibility is to see that each production in a season is completed within the allotted budget. This person also is involved in coordinating schedules and meetings among the different units as each play takes shape.

In some community theater organizations, the production manager assembles the production leaders for each play. Typically, the production manager purchases each play from a publisher or licensing agency. Working with other key individuals, the manager sets the season schedule and secures places for rehearsals and meetings. The manager establishes a budget to cover the costs of each production. Hopefully, by the end of each play's run or shortly afterward, all the expenses will be recovered.

Play Director

The director begins by scheduling **auditions**. Naturally, the main concern is to identify the players who are just right for each part. There are additional considerations, though. For example, can the actor be available for all, or almost all, rehearsals? Is the player easy to get along with? Might there be potential conflicts with other members of the cast or crew? Is the director confident that the actor has a good work ethic and will be a well-rounded asset to the production?

In some companies, the director is given the liberty to select the designers and other key staff members of the production at hand. In others, certain experienced staffers perform the same job in all or most plays throughout the season.

The director makes out the cast rehearsal schedule. This requires coordination. If the theater shares, leases, or borrows space in a building used for other purposes, the facility probably is at the theater's disposal only at certain times—perhaps only at night and on weekends. Set design and construction crews also require scheduled time. So do sound and lighting technicians.

The director also must be mindful of time constraints that affect certain members of the cast. College students taking night classes may be unable to attend rehearsals on certain evenings. Single parents and people who work night or early morning shifts have a similar problem. These factors should be brought to light during the audition/interview process.

For details about the director's responsibilities, refer to *Directing in Theater*, a companion book in this series.

Stage Manager

The stage manager literally runs the presentation from moment to moment. Thomas Schumacher, a

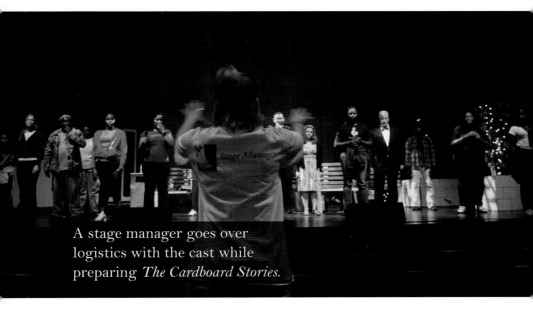

A stage manager goes over logistics with the cast while preparing *The Cardboard Stories.*

noted Broadway producer and author of *How Does the Show Go On?*, describes stage managers as "the lifeblood of rehearsing, running, and maintaining a show." Schumacher surmises that "from the time everyone walks through the stage door to the final curtain, the stage manager is in charge of the production … If you want to know what's going on in a theater, ask the stage manager."

Happily, most theater companies provide the stage manager with a complement of capable assistants. Deputies and assistants are given assignments such as **cueing** and furniture/prop handling.

Set Designer

The set designer arranges everything onstage: **backdrop**, entrances, furniture, window and wall curtains, and hand props (gloves, playing cards, tennis rackets, cigarette lighters, etc.). Thomas Schumacher observes that the set designer creates "everything on the stage except the actors and what they are wearing."

The purchased play materials ordinarily provide floor plans, lists of furniture and props, and images of a completed set. In community and school theaters, however, space limitations may make it impossible to stage the original set. A creative set designer is able to make suitable adjustments—usually by simplification. The designer confers with the director, stage manager, and technical specialists to come up with sets that are attractive, effective, and manageable.

In-depth information about this role is contained in a separate book in Exploring Theater, *Set Design and Prop Making in Theater*.

Costume and Makeup Designers

What an actor is wearing gives the audience immediate clues as to the character's personality. There is a reason for every detail: loud or subdued colors, gaudy or simple designs, ill fits or perfect fits, trendy versus old-fashioned styles.

The costume designer is intimately familiar with the total production. Costumes obviously have to be appropriate to the time period and social setting. They also should help convey the natural ambience the playwright had in mind for each character. The designer not only studies the work carefully but consults with the director, who has the authority to alter certain elements of the script to make the local theater's version of the play unique. The set designer's color scheme also influences costume design.

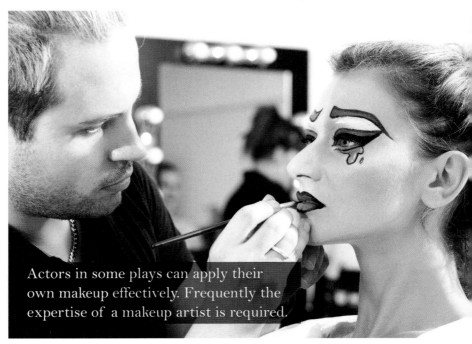

Actors in some plays can apply their own makeup effectively. Frequently the expertise of a makeup artist is required.

Period plays require the designer to conduct research. Designers take special pleasure in creating costumes with realistic historical detail.

Along with the costume, makeup defines each character's physical appearance. In some plays, most of the actors can apply their own makeup. Extreme hair designs and facial, hand, and foot features and deformities may require more than one makeup artist and take hours to apply. The makeup designer decides details of how each character should appear.

A fledgling local theater organization may have only one costume and makeup supervisor. Larger companies may appoint separate costume and makeup designers, each with assistants.

Costume Design in Theater, another volume in this series, describes costume design in detail.

Technical Experts

Effective lighting is absolutely essential for a successful presentation. One scene may need to be bright and colorful. The next may be only partially lit by the dim glow of a lamp or candle. In some scenes, actors perform in two or more small, disconnected areas of the stage that are lit, separated by darkness. Whether the stage is sunny, foggy, or cast in eerie shades, the audience expects to see a set in which all the lighting elements appear natural.

Audio quality also is important, especially if the production is a musical or relies heavily on music and sound effects. Some plays, though, have no musical accompaniment and no particular audio requirements aside from the actors enunciating their lines and projecting their voices.

Lighting and sound directors are responsible for establishing the correct effects. They may require numerous assistants, depending on the play.

Refer to the series volume titled *Lighting and Sound in Theater* for in-depth discussions.

House Manager

Many large community theaters own their facility. Throughout the year, especially during the offseason, they may rent out the building for other uses. These theaters usually designate a house manager (also called a theater manager). The manager might be assisted by a part-time paid or volunteer house staff.

The house manager is responsible for keeping the facility immaculate and pleasing to the public and to the theatrical company, from the décor of the lobby to the cleanliness of the restrooms. During the season, this person is in charge of box office sales and cordially greets members of the audience as they arrive for a performance. If a visitor has a question or complaint that an usher cannot resolve, it is brought to the house manager's attention.

A fundamental responsibility of the house manager is to ensure safety. In case of a fire or other crisis, the manager and the house staff are expected to deal swiftly with the situation. If necessary, they must direct an orderly evacuation. The house manager regularly checks on building security and makes sure emergency exits function properly. This individual enlists, trains, and supervises ushers for every performance. The manager also recruits and supervises people to hand out programs and to staff refreshment and souvenir sales booths.

Hard Work, No Pay

Almost all small theater organizations rely heavily on volunteers. Tight budgets limit the number of participants who can be paid even a small stipend or honorarium. Some community theaters, in fact, operate entirely with volunteers. This provides multiple opportunities for novices interested in testing the theatrical waters. Practically anyone, any age, can find a place in community theater.

Similarly, acting casts in community theaters are mostly or entirely comprised of amateurs. Amateurs act not for pay but because they enjoy it. The experience gives them an opportunity for self-expression, using their creative talents. If they receive payment, they enter the ranks of semiprofessionals or professionals and are no longer considered amateurs.

That isn't to say the amateurs and volunteers who make community theater happen are less dedicated than professionals. They are capable of staging extraordinary productions, and they are driven by a keen determination to do so. They use the same stage tools and require the same talents and skills as theatrical professionals.

Professional actors get their start in school and community productions. Many amateurs hope someday to become professionals. Others have different career interests. To them, theater is an important and rewarding avocation.

Regardless of their long-term ambitions, production personnel in small organizations must have the same essential experience and understanding of the overall process as their professional counterparts. Like the amateur cast and volunteer offstage personnel with whom they work, they are committed to making each show as effective and successful as possible.

All the individuals engaged in theater—production leaders, cast, and crew units—are expected to function as a team. They must be reliable, punctual, and dedicated. For students, committing to theater will mean less time for leisure interests. If they lack discipline, it can impair their schoolwork. For adults involved in community theater, the time demands will impact their homelife and can affect their jobs. Everyone should consider his or her involvement carefully before committing. Once you join the team, other people's lives can be influenced by how well you perform.

This play is being staged at a reconstruction of the Globe Theatre in London. William Shakespeare presented many of his plays at the Globe.

CHAPTER THREE

RANGE OF RESPONSIBILITIES

I t's interesting that in early theater, there was no organized production system. In records concerning the ancient Greek dramas of Aeschylus and Sophocles, historians find no reference to producers or directors. The same is true of Shakespearean dramas and comedies. Playwrights or leading actors were in charge. They often financed productions out of their own pockets.

By the late nineteenth century, individuals with designations such as stage managers and directors were being acknowledged in the credits. By the 1920s, with productions becoming more complex, reviewers recognized their importance in successful productions. Today, teams of well-organized personnel work behind the scenes in community as well as professional theater. They often number more than the players onstage. Production leadership is especially important in small organizations in which many of the volunteer participants are inexperienced.

No single organizational structure applies to every community or school theater group. Large organizations can designate a person with expertise for every position imaginable, from producer to

French actress Silvia Monfort (*center*) leads the cast in a performance of Aeschylus's *The Persians*.

publicist. Small entities, by contrast, do the best they can with the few knowledgeable production people they have. They frequently manage to do very well, delivering presentations that would impress professional critics. For many, there is no such thing as, for example, a lighting designer or house manager.

No matter how the roles are designated, each leader or coordinator has duties to perform throughout the production, from early planning to striking the stage and the premises after the final curtain call. The three basic phases of a theatrical presentation are preproduction, rehearsal, and show time. In each phase, different personnel are more active and have more central responsibilities. Most of the following topics are among the production responsibilities in smaller theater groups.

Launching a Production

Preproduction is what happens before cast rehearsals, set design and construction, costume design, and technical preparations are all set in motion. It begins with selecting the works that will be performed during the season. Once a play is agreed on and the rights and materials are purchased, production leaders study the script closely and formulate—as a team and as specialists—how they will approach the project.

Selecting the Play

The people responsible for play selection have an interesting balancing act to perform. When planning a season schedule, they must come up with a diverse menu that offers their **patrons** drama, suspense, comedy, sorrow, surprise, and music. Companies usually plan a season that includes longtime favorites along with less familiar works. If available, they like to occasionally showcase works by local or regional playwrights.

In selecting plays for the season, other factors also have to be considered. The company should mix plays noted for their sheer entertainment value with more thought-provoking works that are rich in educational value. If the organization expects to meet its budget, box office potential is a concern.

Plays are bought from various publishing and licensing companies. Samuel French, Inc., (http://www.samuelfrench.com) for many years has maintained a huge catalog of available plays. Its FAQ section answers questions pertaining to issues such as editing the script and videotaping the production. Another long-established licensing firm is Dramatists Play Service (http://www.dramatists.com). An organization that focuses on new works is Theatrical Rights Worldwide (http://www.theatricalrights.com).

In selecting each play, the production leaders have to be sure it is a manageable fit for their available resources and is attractive to their patrons. Three considerations are foremost:

The play must be doable, given their staff, roster of regular players, facilities, and equipment. If a play under consideration requires unusual acting talents (actors who have convincing foreign accents, athletic or acrobatic ability), it might be impossible for a local group to stage effectively. If it would require that the company rent or borrow special items or recruit outside stage talent, the producers need to look into those arrangements in advance. A set may require the work of professional carpenters, electricians, and other specialists not regularly involved with the company.

While manageable, it also should be challenging to produce. Cast and crewmembers want to stretch their talents, learn new skills, and broaden their experience with each new play in which they are involved. A play that is too easy to stage will be boring to the company and the audience alike.

In selecting plays for a coming season, production leaders consider multiple factors.

It must appeal to their base of supporters. Presumably, production leaders are intimately familiar with what their subscribers and prospective new attendees within the community like and dislike. Some theatrical communities relish **avant-garde** material. Some have much more traditional tastes. Some have a healthy appreciation for the whole spectrum of theatrical works.

Certain plays are ideal for amateur companies. Others, including most Broadway hits and Shakespearean classics, are too ambitious for a small company to attempt. Very small groups tend to favor one-act plays that have just one set and a handful of players. The advantages are obvious—including simplified rehearsal scheduling.

Many theater veterans believe musicals are the category of play most likely to be hits with community audiences. Jimm Cox, director of theater at the University of South Carolina Upstate, has been involved with various types of theater for many years. While college programs have built-in academic funding that permits them to stage lesser-known, progressive works, community theaters must work continually at fundraising. "As a result, they normally produce a much more commercial season with appeal to a general audience," Cox says. "Musicals often provide the best vehicles for generating ticket sales. They are, however, much more expensive to produce."

Musicals also are more complicated. Success hinges first on whether the cast has outstanding musical talent. A musical is much more involved than other types of plays. It may require a professional

Youth barbershop quartets can enliven theatrical revues.

sound crew. Also, most musicals call for colorful sets and spectacular lighting effects.

Accompaniment is required for the vocalists. Unless a piano suffices throughout the play, a community orchestra or ensemble must be engaged.

Using a soundtrack is an option but is frowned on by many artistic directors.

Musicals typically involve dancing. That means the production needs a choreographer as well as a musical director, in addition to other production leaders.

The Revue: Entertaining and Simple

Musicals present complex challenges to community and school theaters with limited resources. A similar **genre** of production, meanwhile, can be almost as entertaining to the audience, with much fewer demands on the company. It is the revue.

A revue is a miscellaneous program of skits, solo performances, and short musical pieces. There is no plot. It simply presents a colorful variety of performers delivering examples of what they do best. Sketches from famous plays and performances of popular songs can enrich the menu. Intermingled might be episodes that let local performers simply do what they like to do.

The audience is amused. The company's performers are relaxed. However, production issues may be challenging. There will be a relentless sequence of staging, lighting, and audio demands on the crew. Scheduling rehearsals—with a mixed bag of performers, some of whom have little or no theater experience—can be difficult. Certain acts may need unusual equipment and props.

Managing the Production

Community theaters and school theatrical departments may present half a dozen or more plays

A HUMBLE START

Jimm Cox, like most production veterans, traces his earliest theatrical interests to childhood. His own path eventually led to an academic career. He is the longtime director of theater and director of the Foreign Study London program at the University of South Carolina Upstate.

"Like many small town farmer's children, my theater experience began in the church, where I was encouraged to be verbal," he recounts. "My undergraduate degree is in speech education. I was offered a graduate teaching assistantship for public speaking and voice and **diction** in a graduate theater program. Several years of **summer stock** gave me some practical experience."

As a young actor, Cox earned a leading role in a commercial summer production of *You're a Good Man, Charlie Brown*. But acting was not his focus. He began writing, directing, and producing shows for corporations as well as athletic events, including the Pan American Games for the Visually Impaired. Since

in a seven- or eight-month season. The production manager plans, schedules, and coordinates the different phases of each play's preparation and performance for the season. They include design, construction, rehearsal, and performance, as well as various meetings. While one play is in its performance run, the next one may be in rehearsal, while the third might be in the design process.

joining the faculty at USC Upstate, he has taught courses in introduction to theater, theater history, playwriting, acting, directing, and stage movement. Meanwhile, he has directed more than one hundred productions in university, community, and professional theater programs. He also has served as artistic director for the South Carolina Governor's School for the Arts and Humanities. Cox is a member of *Who's Who in American University Teaching*.

Cox's students have rated him "hilarious," "very intelligent," and "awesome" as an instructor—but one who is "very demanding." One posted, "His class is a lot of fun but it is also a *lot* of work ... Oh, and *don't* be late."

"I never wanted to do anything other than teach," Cox reflects of his long career. "Forty-three years later, I was just named the system-wide University of South Carolina Trustee's Professor. Our program is now nationally and internationally recognized."

The manager has contact information for every member of the production staff, cast, and work crews readily available. This person ensures smooth communications throughout the organization. The manager needs a solid understanding of how everything works, from lighting to marketing. Usually, the production manager has years of experience in multiple functions, including acting.

Maintaining the facility also may be the production manager's responsibility. Depending on the size of the company, the manager may have a staff of helpers. In small theaters, the manager may work alone, personally ensuring that the building is kept orderly, safe, and clean.

Casting and Auditioning

Ordinarily in community and school theater, the director selects the cast. Some large organizations have a casting director, who works closely with the play director in making the selections during the audition process.

Auditions are conducted by the director/casting director and typically involve other members of the creative team such as the music director. In some instances, the director already has in mind familiar actors for certain parts—but they still must audition to make sure they are the right choice. Other tryouts are newcomers, completely unknown to the creative staff. Among them may be fledgling actors with astonishing talent.

Some candidates are selected on first audition; some are called back for subsequent auditions. On occasion, an auditioning actor does not seem just right for the part as scripted but is so impressive that the creative team decides it will be worthwhile to make adjustments. They may be willing to let the actor develop a character significantly different from the one the playwright had in mind. They may even let the actor alter some of the lines. (This may require permission from the licensing agency.)

In his book *Theatre Craft*, John Caird points out that the auditioning director or group always should be polite, gracious, and generous to each candidate. "Actors are at their most vulnerable and often their most unnatural in the artificial atmosphere of auditions. They are being asked to respond to material with which they are often totally unfamiliar." He adds, "It is often the most imaginative actors who are the most nervous."

Auditioning for musicals presents special challenges. The audition hall must have "dry" **acoustics**—no echo. Usually a piano is used for accompaniment. It is important to use a pianist who has experience working with tryouts and can put them at ease. Veteran directors cite another essential: the piano must be in tune. Sour accompanying notes distract the singer and distort the rendition.

In university theater productions, casting presents special dilemmas. Jimm Cox at the University of South Carolina Upstate explains, "Age range is often limited, if only traditional university students audition." How, for example, does the auditioning panel deal with children's parts?

Small theater directors often take time to explain to novice actors certain basic rules that veteran actors understand well. Rule One: Always be on time. Additionally, bring paper and pencils to rehearsals for taking notes. Don't come to a rehearsal if you have a cold or flu; transmitting it to others could jeopardize the entire project. Also, don't change your appearance between the time of the audition and the beginning of rehearsals. A common aggravation of directors is for an excited actor who has just landed her first role to appear at the first cast meeting with a dramatic new hairstyle.

Setting the Stage

What the audience will see, apart from the actors, is whatever the set designer creates. The same play produced by a dozen companies will have a dozen unique sets. While the fundamental design is the same, the total picture differs. Variable factors include space limitations, available materials, and—most influentially—the designer's unique ideas and style.

In fashioning the set, the designer works in coordination with the director and stage manager. The designer may need to confer in advance with carpenters, electricians, and other workers. It becomes a multifaceted collaboration when the team must produce completely different sets for different acts—a test that dedicated designers relish. It may be no small challenge for the designer and backstage personnel to work out where to stow sizeable furnishings and props so they can be moved quickly between acts and scenes.

The set designer in larger companies has assistants to secure fixtures, furniture, carpets, and props. In very small community organizations, the designer may have to do it all.

A critical concern that the set designer in any theatrical production constantly keeps in mind is the literal point of view of the entire audience—each person's line of vision when looking at the stage. In a movie, multiple cameras depict every scene from different angles. All film viewers can see and digest exactly what appears, moment by moment, in the foreground and background. In theater, each member of the audience has exactly one vantage point: the location of the seat. The set designer has to arrange all the elements onstage so that wherever a person is sitting in the audience, most or all of the scenery in all of the sets will be in clear view. All ticket-buying theatergoers should feel satisfied that they've enjoyed every element of the show, regardless of the seating.

Controlling and Changing the Stage

Stagehands are drilled to make astonishing alterations between scenes and acts, usually in almost complete darkness. The stage manager coordinates all of the offstage work during the performance and signals the cues for scenic and lighting changes.

The stage manager has to be familiar with every aspect of the production: script, cast, set, costumes, lighting, and everything else. The manager works very closely with the play's director. Among other duties, the stage manager works out the coordination between the artistic and technical elements of the production.

In rehearsal, the stage manager calls the actors and crew together. The manager knows the script as intimately as the director.

Dressing the Cast

Costume designers and their wardrobe staff measure and fit each actor. This usually is done before or during the first few days of rehearsal. Ideally, costumes are based on drawings or photos from professional productions of the play.

Tailors adjust dresses at the workshop of noted costume designer Stefano Nicolao in Venice, Italy.

The best costume designers don't simply research the play, the period, and the common styles of dress worn at that time and place. They work with the cast. They learn details about how the actor envisions playing his or her character. A full tweed suit, circa 1900, may be just what an actor wants in one play. A different actor playing the same role in another production of the play might insist on simply a shirt, bowtie, and trousers, perhaps adding a vest.

The play's director and actors have a say in the ultimate appearance of the costumes. A leading player may be uncomfortable or believe the outfit design is just not right for the character the actor is trying to portray. This can be a distraction that noticeably impacts the performance.

Perfecting the Lights and Sounds

The dual objective of lighting is to properly illuminate the figures—particularly the faces—of the players as well as the set. Lighting a stage set has been compared to painting on a canvas. Some plays call for brilliant lighting effects, others for subtle degrees of illumination to establish a particular mood. For most scenes, the playwright expects the lighting to appear natural, but for certain others, unnatural light lends a captivating effect.

Balancing the lighting effects between people and objects can be difficult. It is not uncommon for the lighting designer, set director, and play director to disagree. The challenges of lighting are especially evident in community theater. The stage and surrounding space usually is constrained, and there probably is limited money available to buy or rent extra lights, reflectors, and other equipment.

In addition to lighting technicalities, many plays involve onstage and offstage sound effects. The services of an experienced sound engineer may be needed.

Musicals and plays that rely heavily on musical content engage a musical director. The musical director chooses and directs musicians and works with sound engineers. A sound designer is appointed in productions that call for multiple sound effects in addition to music. This designer decides what equipment to use and where to place it on and offstage.

Spectacular productions might include **pyrotechnics** and aerial movements. They may require trained **flymen** to work pulleys and ropes. The company may appoint or recruit a technical director to oversee all of the special effects and to find crewmembers with the necessary skills.

Rehearsals: Juggling Acts—
With Complications

Theatrical rehearsals occur in segments. The director, choreographer, and musical director all require rehearsal time. They each need access to the facility during the weeks and months prior to opening night. They also need focused attention and cooperation by everyone involved. The producer must ensure they get what they need.

Before onstage rehearsals begin, the director assembles the selected cast to read the play through, one or more times. During the readings, the director makes notes and preliminary suggestions to the actors.

In stage rehearsals, the director "blocks" the actors and props, positioning them on the set. Using colored tape, chalk marks, and numbers on the stage floor, the director designates where each person and item is to stand or be placed during a scene, and where to move. The initial blocking scheme is likely to change as rehearsals progress. In amateur productions, the director understands that the less movement of players during a scene, the better.

As rehearsals proceed, the director makes adjustments as needed. Actors may have difficulty delivering certain lines effectively, or the interplay between characters onstage does not flow naturally. The positioning of actors or props may not work out quite right. The director has the license to make changes.

Controlling the Calendar and Clock

The person in overall charge of the production must arrange the schedule. This is no simple task, especially since two or even three plays might be in different stages of production simultaneously at any given point during the season.

Several types of rehearsal are scheduled. In a dry tech rehearsal, the stage manager directs the technicians and stagehands through the production from start to finish; no actors are present. A wet tech rehearsal is a technical run-through with the cast and crew. Everyone becomes familiar with entrances and cues.

Directors schedule one or more work-through rehearsals. These progress methodically through a scene, act, or the entire play, with pauses whenever necessary to correct mistakes, clarify what the director wants, and make adjustments. A subsequent run-through rehearsal takes the cast and crew through the play or segment nonstop. There may be a "stagger-through" in between, a run-through with occasional stops for critical discussions and changes.

The dress rehearsal is the final practice before the opening performance. Actors are in full costume and makeup. All scenic elements and props are in place. The rehearsal is complete with lights and sounds. Selected guests—patrons, dignitaries, members of the local media—may be invited to preview the show.

Minding Manners

In professional companies, cast and crewmembers are paid and know they have to execute their jobs satisfactorily—or else. If they repeatedly fail to execute or cause disruptions, they're ousted. Discipline rarely is an issue.

It is not so cut-and-dried in small community programs, in which crewmembers are volunteers and actors are amateurs. Not infrequently in community and school theater, directors and stage managers are confronted with discipline problems. It can be particularly messy in school drama productions. Many rehearsals are scheduled after school in the afternoon or in the evening, when brain-dead students just want to relax and let off a bit of steam.

School and community theater programs sometimes attract certain participants who are much less serious than others. They think nothing of showing up late by five or twenty minutes—or of missing a rehearsal altogether. They chat, flirt, and crack jokes during the rehearsal. For them, involvement in the production is nothing more than a pastime, so why shouldn't they enjoy themselves? What's the point of signing on, they reason, if they aren't to have their fun? This attitude, of course, can drive stage managers and directors bananas.

The solution is to impose standard theater etiquette. The cardinal rules: (1) always be on time, and (2) mum's the word during meetings and offstage during rehearsals.

What? Postpone the Play?

No one can pause the clock. As the opening performance date nears, some productions simply aren't ready for prime time. They may require an additional dress rehearsal. (Some theatrical advisers recommend several dress rehearsals even if the cast and crew are well prepared.) Even then, much work is still required—and certain difficulties may seem insurmountable. Disaster is in the air.

The most difficult decision an artistic director, director, or stage manager ever has to make is to call for a postponement. It isn't unusual, however. As the rehearsal schedule draws to an end, the director may realize the play is not ready for an effective debut. Leading actors may still lack confidence in some of their lines and delivery. Problems with the set, props, or costumes may still be unresolved. The show may appear awkward from start to finish.

Opening night shows always have countless imperfections. That's expected. But if there is a risk of major blunders, the person in charge must decide whether another day or week of preparation is absolutely essential. Wise directors and administrators understand that a disastrous opening night can ruin the whole season and injure the company's reputation for years to come. A postponement will disappoint patrons for the moment, but they will forgive and forget if the delayed presentation is a success. At the same time, it will be a relief to cast and crewmembers who recognize that they are not yet prepared.

Producing in Unusual Environments

Not all plays are presented in traditional theater buildings. In fact, they can be produced practically anywhere. Many young people get their first taste of the challenges as well as the excitement of production by staging plays in garages and on backyard patios.

Two forms of theater have special appeal to audiences and pose unique challenges to producers: outdoor theater and dinner theater. Each requires a different combination of production personnel and skills.

Outdoor theater is popular worldwide. Plays are presented at community festivals, in town parks and gardens, on the lawns of historic homes, beside lakes and rivers, on farms, and even on sidewalks. Outdoor theatrical programs require those familiar with indoor production tasks to adapt their experience. For some productions, they must call in specialists.

Nina Ayres, writing in *Creating Outdoor Theatre: A Practical Guide*, explains: "A relatively small show can be created by just a handful of individuals who cross the divide from one skill to another with ease. Conversely, larger outdoor theatre productions that rely on special effects will need to employ specialists in each area to realize their ambitions safely and effectively."

Outdoor theater producers must bear in mind the variables of nature. Rain and intense summer heat and humidity are obvious constraints. Even a moderate breeze can cause problems for satisfactory sound—or might be exploited for effect, depending on

Outdoor venues pose unique challenges, especially related to lighting, sound, and weather.

the play. The time of day when the show takes place is significant (sunrise or sunset could lend a wonderful touch, or blind the audience).

Available space and the focusing of audience attention on the selected stage area all may be very simple to arrange, or they may present difficulties that require creative solutions. Many of the behind-the-scenes tools and options commonly used in indoor productions are irrelevant. Set design, effective musical performance, and other theatrical components are different outdoors. Technical effects that require electrical power can be problematic.

As in indoor theater, the general manager or production manager usually handles business matters. An artistic director is in charge of the creative aspects. Some outdoor companies, though, designate an overall producer to assume ultimate responsibility for business, artistic, and technical issues.

In some instances, an outdoor presentation may be a labor of love conceived by a theatrical veteran with broad experience in all functions. This person becomes a producer much like cinematic producers. She or he will find funding, buy the play, select the artistic director or play director as well as other key personnel, schedule meetings, and ensure effective communication among everyone involved.

Completely different is the dinner theater scenario. Most dinner plays are produced in restaurants. Sometimes community theaters that have moveable audience seating put on special productions. They set up the viewing area with dining tables and have a meal served to patrons by caterers, either before or during a stage play. Dinner theaters are different from theater restaurants, where the meal is served in a separate room and patrons afterward move into a regular auditorium for the play. Dinner theaters are much more complex to produce.

In many dinner theaters, the stage is in the center of a vast dining room. This changes the whole production approach for the director, set designer, and actors. There is no **downstage**, **upstage**, or side stage. The audience is not watching from one facing direction, but from all around.

At the same time, the position of the stage completely surrounded by tables of diners served

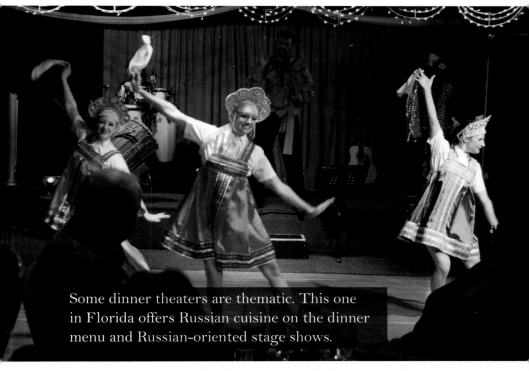

Some dinner theaters are thematic. This one in Florida offers Russian cuisine on the dinner menu and Russian-oriented stage shows.

by moving waitstaff raises mechanical, electrical, audio, and safety issues. The technical crew has to be creative in coping with elements not present in a traditional theater environment.

The restaurant management or catering company necessarily has a major role in production arrangements. Conflicts are not uncommon. Both the theatrical staff and restaurant management generally have to make substantial concessions.

Most dinner theaters are produced professionally, often as a branch of a restaurant business. Some, though, are nonprofit. An example is the Starlight Dinner Theatre in Lansing, Michigan. There, performances and dining take place in an intermediate school cafeteria/auditorium.

Spreading the Word—Constantly

While all of the work is being done throughout the season, a publicity director or staff communicates regularly with print, broadcast, and online media to inform the community about the work of the theatrical company and its upcoming schedule of plays. The company's publicist or media coordinator develops a list of print, broadcast, and online media. This database is updated with changing contact information and notations. The publicist must be in regular communication with the production staff to develop new publicity ideas and angles.

The objective of publicists is to get people's attention and keep the name of the theatrical company and its upcoming production schedule in the public eye. Any development that would be of interest to a significant segment of newspaper readers or broadcast viewers and listeners can be developed into a press release and distributed to the local media. News topics can include the appointment of key staff members, acquisition of new equipment or props, new sponsors, spikes in subscriber growth, etc.

Traditional media—local newspapers and broadcast stations—are still important for theatrical publicity. Publicists not only send out news releases but arrange for print interviews and broadcast appearances with the artistic director, play director, lead actors, and others. Increasingly, companies also use online platforms to share information. They maintain websites, blogs, Facebook pages, and

Twitter accounts. Over time, they amass thousands of followers. The internet makes it simple to communicate with supporters directly, en masse.

In some small organizations, the publicist may serve in the same role as promoter. Ticket sales are the lifeblood of the theater. Advance ticket sales are important. While cast and crewmembers are encouraged to sell tickets in person, the promoter/publicist addresses the community at large.

Aside from the media list, the company maintains lists of current and past subscribers, as well as subscriber prospects. Letters and/or email memos are sent to the lists, inviting ticket purchases. Technology-savvy theatrical companies make it easy for recipients to buy tickets to an upcoming play and/or subscribe as season patrons online, with just a few keystrokes, using a credit or debit card. For supporters who prefer to pay by check, an order blank appears at the bottom of the postal letter.

Publicity and promotion personnel spearhead the growth of formal support groups such as Friends of the Theater. They always are on the lookout for new sponsors. All of these initiatives cost the company little or nothing. Free publicity is vital for amateur theatrical groups to thrive.

Meanwhile, marketers sell advertisements that appear in the playbill of each project. Some advertisers buy single ads for specific shows; others keep a standing ad in every playbill throughout the season. While this work is not integral to the production process, the chief administrative officer, managing director, artistic director, etc., monitor the progress of the promotional efforts.

Show Time!

The days and hours leading up to the opening night performance are exciting and, for most cast and crewmembers, a bit worrisome. In professional theater, opening night disappointment can make for a disastrous run that loses thousands of dollars and devastates careers. In community and school theater, not nearly as much is at stake, and audiences and reviewers tend to be more forgiving. Even the smallest company has its pride, though.

Every actor, even one who excels in his or her performances and duties, is embarrassed by a poor overall presentation. The same is true backstage. If a technical blunder cannot be overcome on the fly, it can spark a chain reaction of consequences that ruins the production.

Even if everyone is well prepared and confident, there is a fear of uncertainty. Unforeseen problems can occur moments before the curtain rises. The company's ability to resolve a crisis on short notice—or no notice—can result in a hit or a flop.

Holding It Together

Ultimately, the director is responsible for what happens in front of the audience. During the performance, the director is literally the boss of the cast. Meanwhile, the stage manager has overall responsibility for almost everything else. If a technical or equipment problem cannot be resolved by the unit leader or crew, the stage manager must come up with a Plan B, on the spot.

In many companies, the stage manager is considered the director's first lieutenant. A period as stage manager, in fact, often is considered a required step toward becoming a director. The stage manager must be thoroughly knowledgeable of each detail, at every progressing moment. This person typically is involved in the "blocking" (positioning onstage) of cast members during rehearsals. If the director must miss a rehearsal, the stage manager should be able to run it. If an illness or accident deprives the production of its director on the eve of performance, the stage manager is the likely substitute.

There are nights when, in spite of everyone's best preparations, things just go wrong. A control panel button is touched accidentally; the ensuing moment of technical confusion results in a missed cue or forgotten line. A similar calamity could occur in reverse: an actor's missed cue could lead to uncertainty offstage as to what should happen next.

At the end of the evening, it may not be an overall successful performance that gives the greatest satisfaction. Rather, it may be the company's pride in maneuvering through a scene that didn't go at all the way it was scripted—with the audience never suspecting anything amiss.

Monitoring the Audience

It was a show guaranteed to please a Saturday matinee audience. The small theater production of *Seven Brides for Seven Brothers* was perfectly cast and inspiringly directed. Every member of the cast performed flawlessly. The set, props, lighting, and sound were perfect. Between scenes, the stage crew maneuvered with methodical precision.

There was one glaring—literally glaring—problem. In the center of the audience sat the leading actress's doting uncle with his digital camera. He was aware of the no-flash-during-performance rule, but he was techno-ignorant. He assumed that as long as he held down the flip-up flash mechanism on his camera, there would be no flash. Every time he pressed the shutter button, though, a split-second glow illuminated the auditorium and stage.

This distraction was addressed firmly but politely, without pointing fingers, during intermission by the

A parent makes a video recording of a child's performance in a school play, blocking the view of others.

master of ceremonies: No photos, please—period. The distraction caused by a camera flash could be dangerous if it occurs at a moment when an actor is making a delicate movement onstage.

The great majority of theatergoers know the rules. From time to time, though, reminders have to be given at intermission—or quietly during an act. Children and teens can be rowdy; an adult or two might arrive inebriated and spontaneously make a loud remark during the performance. The house manager or a member of the production staff may be called in to reinforce an usher.

Snapping photos and taking videos is common at music concerts but not tolerated at plays. Another distraction is eating and drinking—the fizz or snap of a pop-top while opening a drink or the crush of a candy wrapper can be heard for some distance. Patrons at professional theater performances know that the flashes and glows of smartphone cameras and digital cameras cause problems. Community and school productions, though, draw many people who are not so considerate. Relatives and friends are eager to photograph or video record their favored performer's brief moment in the spotlight. They might miss the cautionary statement in the program and the preliminary announcements.

Production leaders train ushers and others in what they might expect. If possible, they should resolve such problems quietly and courteously, without drawing the notice of surrounding members of the audience and without estranging the violator to the theater experience.

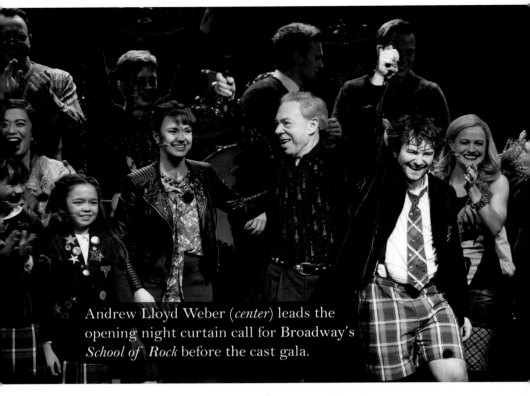

Andrew Lloyd Weber (*center*) leads the opening night curtain call for Broadway's *School of Rock* before the cast gala.

It's Not Over When It's Over

Practically all actors know what to do in curtain calls. A bit of planning may be in order, though, in musicals. In certain musicals, the producer/directors should have a memorable song ready to **reprise**. For enthusiastic viewers, it is icing on the cake. For those who are less appreciative, it hopefully will call to memory the most positive moments of the production.

At the conclusion of the first performance of a run, it's party time! The pressure is off. Cast and crew let off steam and celebrate. The opening night gala typically is joined by financial supporters of the company, local dignitaries, critics, and other selected invitees.

The opening night party provides an opportunity for the hard-working company not only to celebrate but to bond. In her classic book *The Complete Handbook for Community Theatre*, author Jean Dalrymple explains, "Actors who have vowed never to speak to each other again once the play is over may be found at the cast party in each others' arms. The sound effects person and the male lead will be guffawing loudly over the doorbell that never rang … And the director—maligned and whispered about and even cursed through all the weeks of rehearsal—will now be toasted for her pulling together of the impossible dream."

In a London presentation of *The Snowman,* actors take to the air. Aerial and acrobatic scenes present obvious challenges to production crews.

CHAPTER FOUR

PITFALLS AND DIFFICULTIES

Every stage production presents challenges. They often are unique—situations that never occurred before and hopefully never will again. Theatrical production problems stem from a range of causes. A few of the many examples include these:

- Extraordinary staging requirements

- Unusual requirements for props, costumes, lighting and sound, and other elements

- Damage to the building, set, or equipment

- Sickness, injury, or personal crisis resulting in prolonged absences of key personnel

- Personal conflicts among team members

- Budget overruns

Sometimes, production leaders encounter difficulties that could have been avoided if smarter decisions had been made long before the problems occurred. Such decisions may go back to the selection of a play that is above the reasonable capabilities and means of the theater company. Problems that recur throughout a season or over several seasons might be traced to the organization's choice of venue or appointment of certain individuals to permanent staff positions.

Need for Satisfactory Space

The fundamental requirement for a successful theatrical company is securing a suitable home. Community or "little" theater organizations use various facilities for staging their productions. Settings include auditoriums at schools, churches, private business locations, and local government buildings. Theatrical companies might be given the use of the property at no cost. Some organizations acquire, by lease or cheap purchase, vacant structures such as abandoned supermarkets, movie theaters, or rural barns. Others can afford to lease a site that offers extra advantages such as more seating capacity; larger stage and offstage space; ready-to-use lighting and

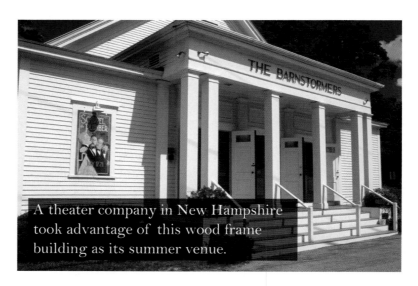

A theater company in New Hampshire took advantage of this wood frame building as its summer venue.

sound equipment; flexible availability of the building for preliminary meetings, work, and rehearsals; easy access and abundant parking for shows; etc.

Ideally, the organization has a long-term arrangement with the property owner. Plans may change, though. Success after a few years may compel the administrators to search for a larger auditorium. Sometimes, the need to change venues is beyond their control. The facility may become unavailable after a contracted season ends—or even during a season—for reasons such as sale or repurposing of the property, fire, or natural disaster. Scrambling to find an adequate new venue and making necessary adjustments can be highly stressful to the whole company (and inconvenient to patrons).

Production Leadership

It is vital for the director and/or casting director to choose the right actors during the auditioning process. But those are the obvious selection decisions. The selection of production leaders can make or break a play or season ... or the company.

Certain production leaders—including the artistic director, production manager, CAO, and house manager—typically are appointed long-term or permanently. Others, such as the play director and set and costume designers, are appointed for specific presentations. It is important to find the best individual for each post. Having to replace a key leader at midseason—or worse, during a production— can be a severe setback.

Reproducing Cinematic Effects

Many modern plays are very ambitious in their production requirements. Some are adaptions of films. Others, while written originally for the stage, demand visual effects no less difficult.

"Shows written in the last ten to fifteen years have become increasingly cinematic and written to be performed at theaters with the budgets and mechanics that only Broadway can handle," explains Jay Coffman, executive artistic director for the Spartanburg Little Theatre. "That means moving to and from fifteen to twenty different locations in one act. *9 to 5: The Musical* was like that. You have to be creative about how you stage those shows. You can't create full sets for each location.

"The musical *Titanic* requires that you create the illusion of something mechanically sinking onstage, which for us was a suspended bridge that ran the length of the stage and tilted as the second act progressed. Also, you have people moving sets—not a mechanical stage setup. Shows like *Mary Poppins* or *Peter Pan*, which require flying effects, add yet another hitch into the production process, and you have to contract outside professional companies who can stage those safely."

When Coffman's little theater decided to present the musical *Titanic*, the production leaders knew it would be a project like no other they had ever attempted. But they had no idea just what was in store.

"*Titanic* proved to be a mammoth undertaking," he says, "and we were rushing to the finish on opening night, due to a number of setbacks on the set-building side. We decided to add some fog/smoke effects on opening night for a scene that takes place in the First Class Smoke Room right before the ship hits the iceberg, which ends act 1. It's a very dramatic moment and song.

"In all our rushing, the fire alarms for the building hadn't been temporarily turned off, which is what usually has to happen. So as the ship was about to hit the iceberg, the lights in the auditorium began to flash and the PA announcement came on advising everyone to leave. But the audience didn't move because they thought it was part of the show. Eventually, they did and we settled everything. They came back and we picked up where we had stopped. It was actually very funny, but felt really tragic on opening night. People still talk about it."

Tim Baxter-Ferguson, director of theater and musical theater at Limestone College, points out that

Starlight Express is one of a growing number of musicals that push the limits in elaborate costuming.

special effects usually are costly—sometimes beyond the production budget. "In our recent production of *9 to 5*, we had to fly an actor in the air. It became clear that we would need to bring in a professional group to handle this in order for the actor to be safe. I, as department chair, had to argue my case to the college president to account for an increase that would be needed in our already tight budget. I made it clear that the safety of the student actor was at stake. We were given the increase."

Jimm Cox, theater head at the University of South Carolina Upstate, adds, "There are often complicated or expensive prop or set pieces that limit production choices. Four period costume shows in a single season would break the bank and exhaust the staff. A full season of demanding and expensive set construction can create unreasonable demands."

"Every production has unique challenges," Baxter-Ferguson observes. "Learning to communicate clearly with all of those involved and understanding their points of view is key."

Juggling School Production Demands

Grade school teachers who lead theater programs face challenges like no one else in theatrical production. Kathy Bradley, an elementary school history teacher and drama leader in Columbia, South Carolina, has been in charge of everything in producing school plays, including script writing. She was given an interesting mission: to involve six classes of third graders in each play, with about twenty-five students per class.

"I had to write each play in six scenes and assign each scene to a class, so we could rehearse just that scene during their regular class time," she explains. "Then, we gathered all classes in the cafetorium for rehearsals of the whole show put together. I needed backstage helpers, either parents or older students, so contacting these people and getting them to commit ahead of time was very important."

Her biggest challenge, she says, was to come up with scripts that gave most of the student actors speaking roles, either individually or in groups speaking together. A recurring challenge was producing a third-grade history play every year for seventeen years—and other plays in other subjects at three other grade levels. One year, a science teacher wanted a play about bats. "I had to think of how to handle costuming, scenery, and storyline for *Bats*."

Scheduling, she notes, can be tricky for classes in lower grade levels. "Getting enough rehearsal time in a school setting where kids *must rehearse during school hours* is tough. One fifty-minute drama class a week is not enough as we start to put the show together, and we have to schedule more rehearsals. It steps on teachers' other classes and they get crabby about that."

Special effects present trials of their own. "When something has to disappear from stage in a magic puff of smoke, you have to get pretty inventive to make it effective on a cafeteria stage."

In time, Bradley received a wonderful reward for her diligence. South Carolina Educational Television redeveloped one of her history plays as a video series.

TRAUMA BACKSTAGE

Much of the drama that occurs in theatrical production has nothing to do with the play script. It happens unexpectedly, in real life, among the cast and crewmembers. It is especially likely to occur in school productions.

Elementary school theater leader Kathy Bradley is quite familiar with young actors experiencing nosebleeds and throwing up. "You grab a towel and try to talk the children 'down' so they can go out and do their parts. One of my students came down with a high fever one night, but she had a leading role, so she'd walk offstage after her lines, and I had a special chair set up for her to rest. Her mother stood back there with an icepack on her head between her scenes."

Showdowns emerge when two or more students want the lead part in a play. "I had two girls who wanted to be Dorothy in *Wizard of Oz*," Bradley recalls. "One of them could sing very well; the other could not. And of course, we had to do 'Over the Rainbow.'"

Bradley cleverly worked out a way for *both* girls to be Dorothy. She wrote a prelude to the play in which an elderly Dorothy (the non-singer) sat reminiscing with Scarecrow about her childhood adventure. The scene closed with her screeching the famous lines of the song in a craggy "old lady" voice. That led into the beginning of the well-known play.

"It was perfect for her," Bradley remembers. "The children were happy. Their parents were happy. It all worked out."

Managing Tension and Dissension

Most people involved in theater are dedicated to doing their part in making a production the best it can be. Whatever their assignment, on or offstage, they take pride in their effort. They understand the importance of working in harmony as a unit.

A troublesome minority of famous, highly gifted professional actors have negative reputations—most commonly, huge egos or irresponsible work ethics. The same is true of certain production professionals. They are in great demand because of their talents, but they are difficult to work with. Bad apples of this sort also are found in some little and school theater organizations.

Preparing and staging a play often can become very intense, even among a full company of cooperative, selfless individuals. As curtain time nears, relationships between long-time friends can become strained to the breaking point. Clashes can disrupt rehearsals. They can result in embarrassing mistakes during a performance, glaringly obvious to the audience.

Part of the creative director and other production leaders' job is to control tempers and avert conflicts. Seasoned directors and managers come to know well the personality characteristics of the regulars involved in their organization. They make assignments carefully, bearing in mind that certain individuals always collaborate well together while other matchups could prove troublesome. The more amiable the pairings and groupings, the less risk of disastrous personality problems as show time approaches.

Safety—Always a Concern

Safety issues naturally come to mind in productions that involve onstage acrobatics, flying scenes, and collisions. Popular examples include *Tarzan, Peter Pan,* and *Mary Poppins.* The flymen who work the ropes, wires, and pulleys to lift, lower, and zoom actors through the air are trained and experienced. Riggers take great care in engineering and setting up equipment properly.

Everywhere, precautions are necessary. A theater is a very busy place, especially during the rehearsal and performance steps. Electrical cables and other extended cords must be taped flat to the

Electrical cords and other wires should be taped flat to prevent tripping. Safety is a constant concern in theatrical productions.

floor to prevent tripping. Cast and crewmembers know to be constantly alert. Apart from the stage itself, most of the building always is in almost total darkness during a performance. Particularly dangerous are the dim-lit wings. There, where actors stand before making their entrances, scenery and furniture is stowed. Between sets, workers must move items on and off the stage very quickly. Some objects—pianos and couches, for example—are quite heavy and unwieldy to maneuver.

During performances, the house manager has overall responsibility for the safety of patrons in the audience. In groups of all sizes and staffing levels, the ushers should be trained in reacting to crises.

Outdoor theater may involve unique safety issues such as audience access to and within the stage and seating area. First aid must be available. Outdoor productions that incorporate fireworks call for additional safety measures.

An Ongoing Difficulty: Finding Money

Many small theater groups operate on a shoestring. No one is paid, and they basically "beg, steal, or borrow" the facilities, equipment, and costumes they need. Others are able to raise thousands of dollars each season to support annual operating budgets that run to five or even six figures.

The primary sources of funding for community theater programs are ticket sales for each production, season memberships, corporate and individual sponsorships, and—for regional and larger community groups—grants. Everyone in the organization is expected to help promote the effort personally through ticket sales, word-of-mouth advertising, and involvement in promotional campaigns. Obtaining paid sponsorships by local businesses and individuals calls for a bit of marketing expertise. Theatrical companies whose leaders believe they qualify for government, local agency, or corporate grant support usually engage a professional grant writer. Each avenue of fundraising comes under the oversight of the organization's administrator or administering committee.

Money for high school drama departments partly is allocated as a **line item** in the school's annual operating budget. The department's share of the overall budget depends on the school's arts education rating and approved curriculum. The amount rarely is more than a small fraction. In many schools, the drama program receives only a token sum.

To help offset expenses and raise money for future productions, middle and high schools typically charge admission to performances. Some confidently charge five dollars, ten dollars, or more at the door, reducing prices for tickets bought in advance.

Kathy Bradley recalls her years as an elementary school drama teacher in South Carolina: "My school would allow me $100 or so, maybe a little more, and I scrounged for cardboard and other prop material at thrift stores and neighborhood trash piles. (Old shutters and louvered doors are *fabulous* set pieces.) I drew paper doll-type diagrams of the costumes for each actor (usually about 150 children—God, those nights were long) and told parents to go to thrift stores to find things that would fit the drawings as best they could. I provided costumes for kids whose parents couldn't come through with one.

"For my purposes, this actually resulted in a very sweet 'kid friendly,' homemade, but also coordinated look. My fifth-graders made video movies, and we actually had a Brennen School 'World Premiere' night. Thinking back on it, we could have sold tickets for all the parents and families who showed up to add to the fund for drama productions. We had a 'red carpet' photographer, and kids dressed up pretty snazzy."

Theater departments at most colleges and universities enjoy, to a great extent, the unique benefit of financial freedom. Tim Baxter-Ferguson at Limestone College explains, "Colleges depend more on tuition contributions and less on ticket sales. Colleges and universities tend to have nicer sets and costumes than smaller theaters because they do not have to be profitable to survive."

Academic theaters do contribute to their own funding support. They produce revenue with ticket sales, concession sales, and other incentives. Jimm Cox at the University of South Carolina Upstate adds, "Most every academic theater works hard to capture donations from friends of the program. Donations of materials, costumes, and properties also contribute to the financial security of college and university theaters. Sometimes, grants supplement the regular operating budget as well."

A technician overlooking the stage practices spotlighting an area where attention will focus during a play. People with technical and carpentry skills are vital in theater.

CHAPTER FIVE

LEARNING EXPERIENCE

In the introduction to his book *How Does the Show Go On?*, Broadway producer Thomas Schumacher provides a broad definition of theater. "It is a business, it is a hobby, it is a place to go to work, a place to play with your friends, a place to learn about yourself, and a place to learn about others. Theater can take place at school, in your garage, in a big fancy building, or even outside in the open air."

In each of those settings, practically everyone who has become involved in theater has benefited in one or many ways. Later in life, successful people in business administration and management, government leadership, health care, manufacturing, professional services, trades, and all other career fields can look back and realize how theatrical participation while a student helped prepare them. Many are still deriving benefits as they take part in little theater productions as an avocation.

Getting a Start in Theater

Participation in school theater programs is the logical first step for students at any grade level who are interested in learning about theater, perhaps with a view toward an avocation or even a career. Meanwhile, exciting opportunities may await them off campus. Community theaters constantly need child actors. Most community theater leaders are more than willing to introduce young people to every aspect of production, from set and costume design to technical work.

Kathy Bradley, a retired elementary school drama producer, avidly encourages young people to become involved in theater. The sooner they start, the better.

"Take any opportunities that are offered to perform or help backstage in school, church, or community theater," she advises. "They should begin *anywhere* they can, even if it's helping their old kindergarten teacher do make-up and costumes or handle crowd control for a preschool play. They can ask their parents to take them to a play at the local high school or little theater, to experience live theater as an audience member. They can sign up for summer camps offered by community theaters, colleges, or universities that host various classes for kids."

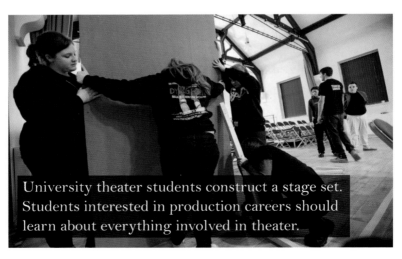

University theater students construct a stage set. Students interested in production careers should learn about everything involved in theater.

Bradley notes that school theater programs frequently introduce students to creative interests they never imagined before. "One boy was *never* interested in participating in drama class, grades one through five, until we started our 'video movie production' unit. I allowed them to pick the jobs they each wanted: makeup artist, costumer, set design, actor, camera operator, sound tech, etc. He signed up for set design.

"Once we all came up with the idea for a script for our short movie, they would begin turning my classroom into their 'set.' He started coming in every day at recess, all animated and excited, and saying things like, 'I thought I'd go ahead and hang this backdrop so it won't take so long to get started shooting this afternoon.' He would drag my ladder over and start staple-gunning away! He'd say, 'Ms. Seibles has a rocking chair in her room. It'll look great for the scene tomorrow. I'll go down and ask her if we can borrow it.'

"I had never seen a kid's energy change so much. Behind the scenes was his thing—and I'd never known it, because we did mostly acting exercises in my elementary classroom. Just goes to show you how beautiful it is when a young person feels interested and empowered by an activity. I hope he found something like that somewhere else in his future."

Extra tips from Bradley for students: "Watch the Academy Awards and see the film clips for makeup, costumes, special effects, sound awards, etc. Read theater magazines, which show lots of good makeup and other techniques. Visit theater supply stores. Watch YouTube demonstrations of makeup, costuming, scenery."

Students discover many benefits from theatrical participation. Typical are Chelsea and Austin Pham and their cousin Andy Hoang, all students at Prairie High School in Vancouver, Washington. Each of them entered the school's theatrical program as freshmen. All three enjoy acting. Andy and Austin also have performed technical tasks, including the setting, focusing, and programming of lights, and handling the fly system to move objects on and offstage.

Joann Tran, Andy's mother, observed that their involvement in school theater has led them to develop their talents in music and dance. It also has nurtured their appreciation for teamwork and interdependence with others. "They get to trust and know people they work with because the environment forces you to be the real you," she said in an interview for this book.

The rewards extend beyond the school campus, she pointed out. "They also learn to balance and manage their time for work, school, and out-of-school activities. They are a family there, and the people who Andy, Austin, and Chelsea are with keep one another out of trouble."

Chelsea is interested in a professional acting career and plans to study theater in college. Austin hopes to become an animator or voice actor. Andy is "just doing theater for the fun"; his career interest is engineering. All three expect to be active in community theater.

Limestone College's Tim Baxter-Ferguson has basic advice for young people interested in theater for fun or as a possible occupation: "Do as much theater as you can, and at as many places as you can. Don't just act onstage, or, if you're shy, don't just do tech. Work lights, costumes, help paint, sit on books, sweep and

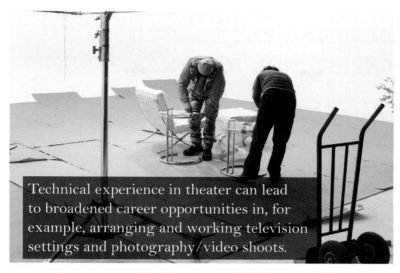

Technical experience in theater can lead to broadened career opportunities in, for example, arranging and working television settings and photography/video shoots.

mop—just get to the theater and help as much as you can. The only way to really learn how theater works is to be involved in as much of it as you can."

Production and Creative Leaders Reflect

Looking back, veteran little theater producer Jay Coffman can trace a sequence of events in his life that led to where he is now: executive artistic director of the Spartanburg Little Theatre. "I grew up doing theater, but never considered doing it professionally. Locally, I became involved here [at the Spartanburg Little Theatre] and worked for a number of years as a volunteer board member. When our executive director left and we were not financially able to hire someone full time, I said that I would help work in the office over the summer when I wasn't teaching college (which is my other full-time job). Eventually, that morphed into a full-time position as our financial standing and

APPLYING THEATRICAL EXPERIENCE TO OTHER CAREERS

Experience in school and in small community theater productions can benefit a person in practically every career field. It can help build stronger communication, collaboration, and problem-solving traits. In some professions, theatrical experience literally is evidenced in daily work.

Jay Coffman reflects, "A number of years ago, a young lawyer became involved in our theater, first taking a small part in one of our musicals, and increasingly taking larger supporting roles and lead roles. The comment has been made by judges and fellow lawyers that his confidence and public speaking ability dramatically increased very rapidly due to his involvement in the theater."

Elementary school drama teacher Kathy Bradley has leveraged her school theatrical experience to further other career goals. "I realized as I moved through my

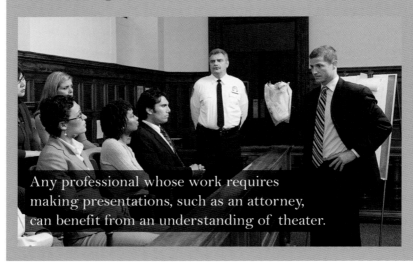

Any professional whose work requires making presentations, such as an attorney, can benefit from an understanding of theater.

seventeen years [in school theater] that I have a knack for writing for children. I tried to make the plays fun for them and their parents, with humor sprinkled in when possible, while creating plots to address our academic subject matter. When I had the chance to rewrite one of my school plays for SC-ETV, I realized this is something I want to do as my next career.

"Also, I am an artist and have sketched several children's books. Theater helped loosen me up and take chances with my writing, and to get great experience knowing and writing for children. It's pretty amazing how a path can wander to a place you really enjoy."

Thousands of adults can look back on various roles in theatrical production that have helped them in all sorts of professions. "It is a remarkable experience for anyone who will get involved," Bradley says.

reputation improved. So I was just sort of at the right place and the right time. I'm still learning.

"Most important, I think, is to consider your community, consider your resources, consider your abilities, and work within them—but always push forward, push the boundaries incrementally. Don't assume your audience is of one mind or of one taste. Provide opportunities for different audience types and differences in your acting pool. Stagnancy will get you nowhere."

Leslie Hendon, a gifted singer, has performed leading roles in Spartanburg Little Theatre productions of *Cabaret* and *Seven Brides for Seven Brothers*. She has played dozens of small parts in other shows. She and her husband, Trey, both have been involved in theater since childhood. They met during the company's production of *Wizard of Oz*.

"Neither of us had big roles—he was a 'winky' and I was a 'poppy,'" she jokes. "So we had a lot of time to talk backstage. If you can fall in love with someone by wearing a green lamé, that says a lot."

Leslie is enthralled by the creative side of theater. She loves to act and sing. She also has functioned as choreographer and stage manager. Trey usually serves as a sound technician. He holds degrees in communication arts and computer science.

From Backstage to Big Screen

Carlos Knight learned the ropes of theater and show business while a middle school student participating in drama programs in Columbia, South Carolina. Like most theatrical students, he gained experience in various production roles. Ultimately, he focused on acting. He landed roles with the city's Town Theater, and at age twelve he began performing in South Carolina ETV productions.

Knight soon was signed by a film agent and moved to Los Angeles, California. He got several television and movie roles. His most important break was a guest appearance in an episode of *ER* in 2008, which earned him a Young Artist Award for Best Performance.

His former drama teacher, Kathy Bradley, remembers Knight's early development as a student. "Carlos was one of my sweetest kids. He just loved theater and threw himself in totally to each assignment and play. He did theater in middle school, community theater, and then told his mom he was serious about theater and

Actor/singer Carlos Knight got his start in entertainment while in grade school.

wanted to move to LA. She was a single mom with another child, but off they went, and Carlos got an agent and started doing a few commercials and some modeling. Then he auditioned for an episode of *ER* and won an award. He was then approached about taking a major role on a new series on Nickelodeon. It was a rocking hit for three or four years. He also started writing and recording rap music with some of the money he made."

Anyone Can Benefit From Theater

From communication-skill development to technical learning, theater offers an exciting field of inspiration for students and adults alike. Mastering production responsibilities and techniques can be valuable for individuals entering any career field.

University theater program head Jimm Cox explains, "Students who train in theater, for the most part, develop exceptional communication skills. Even technicians must communicate script analysis and design concepts. The concepts of team building and ensemble effort provide a universal skill set. We have former students now in public relations, advertising, television, law, and politics. All of these vocations require adaptive, conscientious, diligent, compassionate citizens.

"Theater uses the lessons of the past without being limited by them. It forces us to identify and recognize ourselves, both for our beauty and our flaws. It allows us to project the possibilities for a future free of the limitations that have defined our past."

Kathy Bradley emphasizes that acting at an early age is particularly beneficial. "I have had so many former students come up to me in restaurants, on the street, and tell me how much playing the improv games in drama helped them learn to think on their feet in many situations, and helped them overcome some of their shyness. They comment that being onstage in front of a large crowd, and having received practice and tips to handle those situations, has helped them in public speaking later, in college or in front of colleagues for a business presentation."

A particularly rich platform of learning, if available, is children's theater. Many elementary, middle, and junior high school students have benefited from their experiences. Children's theater organizations are active in all major cities and in many smaller cities and towns. Some offer children not just opportunities to taste the excitement of acting and working backstage, but also serious training in theatrical work.

The Children's Theatre of Charlotte in North Carolina, as one example, provides a broad variety of training programs, camps, residencies by visiting specialists, internships, and jobs. Programs are available for children as young as two years old, and program scholarships are available for students and families of limited means. Activities are scheduled year round.

While many of the programs and projects focus on acting, others involve participants of all ages in diverse aspects of theater, from playwriting and technical training to fundraising. Elementary students learn about theatrical concepts, rehearsing, and public-speaking techniques. Students in grades six to twelve can take master classes, studying related subjects including dance, masked theater, storytelling, songwriting, and circus arts. Campers are caught up in the excitement of producing a show and presenting it on the final day of camp.

Offstage Opportunities

Most high school students who decide to enroll in college theatrical programs have professional acting in mind. However, Jay Coffman, executive artistic director of the Spartanburg Little Theatre, urges them to consider other aspects of theater. He observes, "Everyone wants to be an actor, but I think the real job security is on the production side—stage management, lighting, sound. These types of professionals are always needed, especially if they're good."

Jimm Cox, director of the theater curriculum at the University of South Carolina Upstate, agrees. "We often say that lots of people want to be in the spotlight, but few want to run that spotlight. There are really good jobs in the theater for great technicians—with more positions available to capable women than ever before."

Cox's advice to young people: "For students interested in technical theater and production, get busy! Volunteer and build a résumé. Be creative. Be disciplined. Make yourself an essential part of the technical team. Learn every position and perfect every skill. Demonstrate your ability to be part of a creative team or ensemble. Show that you know when and how to lead and to follow. Sweep, paint, clean the toilets. Do what needs to be done. Be the first to volunteer. Do it well."

The US Bureau of Labor Statistics, in its *Occupational Outlook Handbook*, details career prospects in hundreds of fields. Particularly lucrative are jobs as managers, marketers, electricians, carpenters, and painters. Many of those professionals find work in theater.

Practically all producers in professional theater began by working at side stage and backstage as youngsters. A noted example is British producer Cameron Mackintosh. When he was eight years old, an aunt took him to a musical, and he decided immediately that he wanted theater to be his career. As a teenager, he found work as a stagehand at Drury Lane in London. Then he began working with touring plays. He served as stage manager in *Oliver!* and other professional productions in the 1960s and 1970s. Mackintosh went on to become world renowned and was knighted by Queen Elizabeth in 1996.

Tim Baxter-Ferguson observes, "All theatrical skills apply to the real world. You learn to deal with a large group of people from a variety of backgrounds

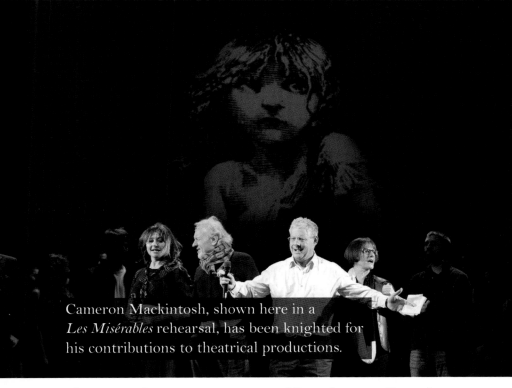

Cameron Mackintosh, shown here in a *Les Misérables* rehearsal, has been knighted for his contributions to theatrical productions.

who are trying to create a magnificently complicated product—the play! You have to communicate, problem solve, be aggressive when needed, but learn to compromise. Not to mention learning to speak in front of crowds, learning to use power tools, and learning to be tolerant."

Veteran participants in all aspects of school and community theater take their work very seriously. They strive to always deliver their finest efforts, offstage and on. At the same time, they share an important philosophy: theater should be fun. At the end of a run, everyone involved should be able to reflect positively on what was accomplished and treasure the memories for the rest of their lives.

GLOSSARY

acoustics Features of an auditorium or smaller room that affect the qualities of sounds as they are heard.

audition Tryout of an actor, singer, or dancer for a certain part in a play.

avant-garde New and unusual ideas, especially in experimental theater.

avocation Secondary time commitment, not a career; hobby.

backdrop Painted cloth or curtain hung across the back of a stage.

budgeting A detailed balancing of production expenses against anticipated income.

commercial Professional, for-profit theater, unlike nonprofit community and school theater programs.

cueing Sending a signal to performers and stagehands to carry out certain actions at predetermined instants.

curriculum Prescribed set of courses in a focused area of study in secondary school or college.

curtain calls Sequence of appearances by actors at the end of a play, acknowledging audience applause.

diction Style of pronunciation of words when speaking or singing.

downstage The front of the stage, closest to the audience.

flymen Trained stagehands who lift, lower, or float actors around the stage using a system of pulleys, ropes, and cables.

genre Category of play defined by its content, style, and/or form.

licensing Granting legal permission for a theatrical company to produce a purchased play.

line item Budget entry showing exactly how much money is allocated for a specific expense.

patron Someone who provides regular financial support to a theatrical company.

prop Short for "property"—a physical item that is placed or carried onstage and becomes part of the scene.

pyrotechnics Fireworks or torches used during a production.

reprise To repeat a song or portion of a popular piece of music for the audience after the play ends.

rigger Worker who equips a set with special gear.

summer stock Theatrical programs that are produced only during the summer offseason.

upstage Area of the stage most distant from the audience.

venue Location of a theater or performance.

FOR MORE INFORMATION

Books

Ayres, Nina. *Creating Outdoor Theatre: A Practical Guide*. Ramsbury, Marlborough, UK: The Crowood Press Ltd., 2008.

Caird, John. *Theatre Craft: A Director's Practical Companion From A to Z*. New York: Farrar, Straus and Giroux, 2010.

Dalrymple, Jean. *The Complete Handbook for Community Theatre: From Picking the Plays to Taking the Bows*. New York: Drake Publishers Inc., 1977.

Gloman, Chuck, and Rob Napoli. *Scenic Design and Lighting Techniques: A Basic Guide for Theatre*. Burlington, MA: Focal Press, 2013.

Hartnoll, Phyllis, editor. *The Oxford Companion to the Theatre*. Oxford, UK: Oxford University Press, 1983.

Mamet, David. *Theatre*. New York, NY: Farrar, Straus and Giroux, 2010.

Schumacher, Thomas. *How Does the Show Go On? An Introduction to Theater*. New York: Disney Editions, 2007.

Volz, Jim. *How to Run a Theatre: A Witty, Practical and Fun Guide to Arts Management*. New York: Back Stage Books, 2004.

Online Articles

Davenport, Ken. "What Does a Broadway Producer Do? Over 100 Producers Respond." *The Producer's Perspective*. https://www.theproducersperspective.com/my_weblog/2010/05/what-does-a-broadway-producer-do-over-100-producers-respond.html?nabe=5407561571893248:0&utm_referrer=https%3A%2F%2Fwww.google.com%2F.

Longwood University Theatre. "Production Handbook." Longwood University, Farmview, VA. http://www.longwood.edu/assets/communication/Theatre_Production_Handbook.pdf.

"Theatre Production Manager: Duties, Outlook and Requirements." Study.com http://study.com/articles/Theatre_Production_Manager_Duties_Outlook_and_Requirements.html.

"What Is the Job Description of a Theater Production Manager." Learn.org. http://learn.org/articles/What_Is_the_Job_Description_of_a_Theater_Production_Manager.html.

Organizations

American Alliance for Theatre & Education
http://www.aate.com
An organization that believes in the transformative power of theater. It provides a wealth of resources for educators, scholars, and others interested in getting involved in the theater arts.

American Association of Community Theatre
http://www.aact.org
Community theaters can access information in a range of topics to help their productions be an enjoyable experience for participants and patrons.

INDEX

Page numbers in **boldface** are illustrations. Entries in **boldface** are glossary terms.

ABOUT THE AUTHOR

Daniel E. Harmon is the author of more than one hundred books on multiple subjects: international and cultural studies, history, biographies, health sciences, government, sports, and career guides. He has written thousands of articles for magazines and newspapers, including performing arts features and reviews for *Music Journal, Renaissance,* and the *New York Times* Arts and Leisure section. Harmon also writes historical mystery fiction. He lives in Spartanburg, South Carolina.